Use your stickers to illustrate the story.

And these are for fun!

I am a frog!

By Camilla de la Bedoyere

Miles
Kelly

Look out for the 'Ask for help!' boxes. You will need help from an adult to do these activities.

Ask for help!

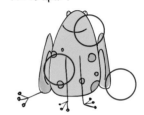

Answers from pages 16–17

Tell us apart

Rhyme time
dog, fog, log, clog

Count me in
5

Who caught the fly?
Florence

True or false?
1. False – it is called a tadpole
2. False – they bellow to attract a mate
3. True.

First published in 2012 by Miles Kelly Publishing Ltd
Harding's Barn, Bardfield End Green, Thaxted, Essex, CM6 3PX, UK
Copyright © Miles Kelly Publishing Ltd 2012
This edition published in 2014

10 9 8 7 6 5 4 3 2 1

Publishing Director Belinda Gallagher
Creative Director Jo Cowan
Editorial Director Rosie Neave
Designer Jo Cowan
Image Manager Liberty Newton
Production Manager Elizabeth Collins
Reprographics Stephan Davis, Anthony Cambray, Thom Allaway

ISBN 978-1-78209-506-4

Printed in China

British Library Cataloguing-in-Publication Data
A catalogue record for this book is available from the British Library

ACKNOWLEDGEMENTS

The publishers would like to thank Mike Foster (Maltings Partnership), Joe Jones, and Richard Watson (Bright Agency) for the illustrations they contributed to this book.

All other artwork from the Miles Kelly Artwork Bank.

The publishers would like to thank the following sources for the use of their photographs:
t = top, b = bottom, l = left, r = right, c = centre,
bg = background, rt = repeated throughout

Cover (front) Ocean/Corbis, (back, tr) EQiuJu Song/Shutterstock, (back, cl) Photography/Shutterstock, Designs & Art/Shutterstock, Richard Peterson/Shutterstock
Corbis 15(r) Michael & Patricia Fogden
FLPA 5(b) Foto Natura Stock; 10 Scott Linstead/Minden Pictures; 13 Michael & Patricia Fogden/Minden Pictures
iStock 8–9(bg) Ewa Mazur
Nature Picture Library 11(tr) Stephen Dalton
Shutterstock Joke panel (rt) Irzik; Heading panel (rt) cristi180884; Learn a Word panel (rt) iaRada; 1 JGade; 2 Envita; 4–5(m) Anneka; 5(tr) Lobke Peers; 6 Brian Lasenby; 7(l) Roger Meerts, (br) Shane Kennedy; 8(panel tr) Anna Ts, (musical notes) Tracie Andrews, (speech bubble) tachyglossus; 9(frog panel r) Okuneva Tatiana, (fruit stickers) Andra Popovici; 11(b) Eric Isselée; 12–13 Cathy Keifer; 14(t) Statsenko, (l) Stefan Fierros, (b) Matej Ziak; 15(c) Dr. Morley Read; 16(t,bg) donatas1205, (t) Stephanie Lirette, (b) LittleRambo; 17(t, bg) TinyFish, (bl) Kakigori Studio, (cr) Elena Kalistratova; 19(t) EcoPrint, (b) Statsenko; 20 worldswildlifewonders; 21(t) Eric Isselée, (b) Steve Bower

Every effort has been made to acknowledge the source and copyright holder of each picture. Miles Kelly Publishing apologizes for any unintentional errors or omissions.

Made with paper from a sustainable forest

www.mileskelly.net
info@mileskelly.net

Contents

I am a frog!

I am a kind of animal called an amphibian. Amphibians can live in water and on land. We lay eggs and like living in wet places.

Large eyes

Long toes

There are more than 5000 different types of frog!

Frog: Meet my friend, Tiny.
Toad: Why do you call him Tiny?
Frog: Because he's my newt!

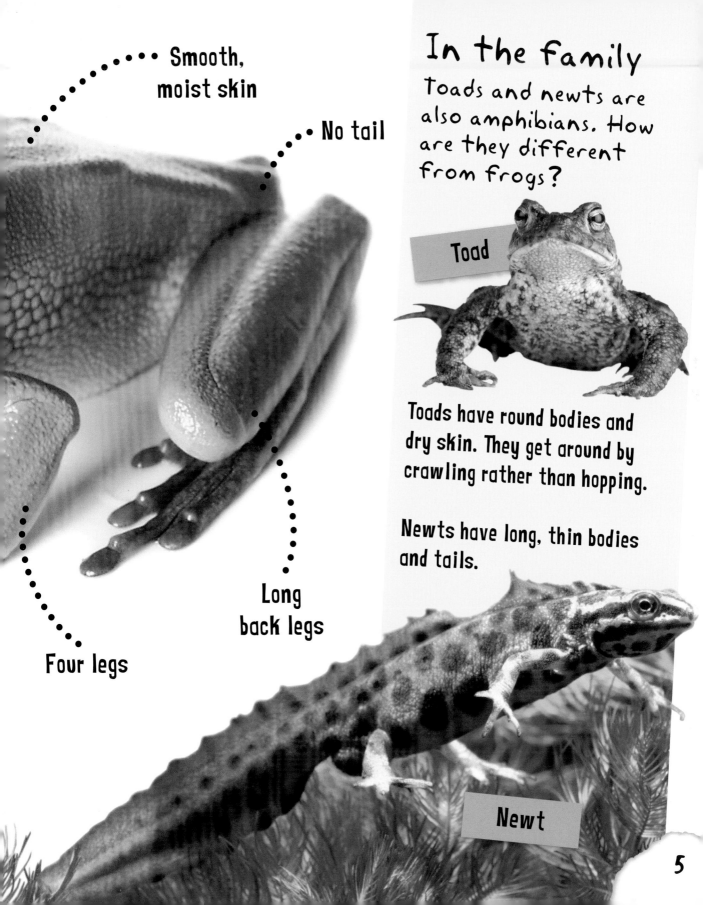

Smooth,
moist skin

No tail

Four legs

Long
back legs

In the family

Toads and newts are
also amphibians. How
are they different
from frogs?

Toad

Toads have round bodies and
dry skin. They get around by
crawling rather than hopping.

Newts have long, thin bodies
and tails.

Newt

Where do you live?

I live on the ground.

My skin is green and brown to help me hide under plants. I stay near water because my skin has to be moist.

·······• Toe pads

Sticky!

Some frogs live in trees. They have sticky pads on their toes that help them to climb.

Q. What is green and slimy and found at the North Pole?

A. A lost frog!

Keeping warm

Some frogs have a winter sleep called hibernation. They hide under rocks or leaves and don't come out until spring.

Activity time

Get ready to make and do!

Croaky contest

Which of your friends can make the best frog noise? Give points for the most realistic, silliest, loudest and croakiest.

Draw me!

YOU WILL NEED: pencils · paper

1. Draw two squashed circles to make your frog's head and body.

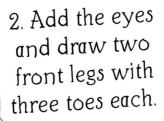

Now colour me in and give me a name!

2. Add the eyes and draw two front legs with three toes each.

3. Give your frog back legs and a wide mouth.

Handy frog

Ask for help!

YOU WILL NEED:
paper plate · green paint
paintbrush · white paper or thin card
scissors · black felt-tip pen · sticky tape

Ask for help!

Yummy green smoothie

HERE'S HOW:

1 Paint one side of the plate green and leave to dry.

2 Make two green hand prints on a piece of paper or card and leave to dry.

3 Cut out the hand prints and tape them to the back of the plate.

4 Cut two 'eyes' from the paper or card and tape at the top of the plate.

5 Draw the frog's features with the pen.

YOU WILL NEED:
2 peeled kiwis
1 peeled frozen banana
120 ml vanilla yogurt
a splash of milk
1 tsp honey
a few drops of green food colouring

HERE'S HOW: Put all the ingredients into a blender and blend until smooth. Serve in a chilled glass. Delicious!

How far can you jump?

I can jump a long way!

I jump to get away from animals that might eat me. The African sharp-nosed frog can jump 5 metres in one giant leap!

Strong back legs

Jump

Flying frogs

Frogs don't have wings, but some seem to fly. They leap from trees and glide to the ground.

Webbed toes catch the air • • • • •

Glide

Q. What kind of shoes do frogs wear?

A. Open-toad sandals!

Swim

Super swimmers

All frogs have long legs and most have webbed feet to help them swim fast.

What do you eat?

I love to eat bugs!

But I will eat almost anything I can catch. I gobble up spiders, worms, slugs, snails and even small fish.

Q. Why are frogs always happy?
A. They eat whatever bugs them!

Fast food

Good eyesight helps a frog to spot bugs. Then its long tongue shoots out to catch them.

Frogs don't chew their food – they don't have any teeth!

A mouthful of mouse

A horned frog can catch a mouse or lizard and swallow it in one gulp!

Down it goes

When a frog swallows food it rolls its eyes. The eyes move down and help push the food into the frog's throat!

13

What are your babies called?

My babies are called tadpoles.

Frog

Frogspawn

1 The eggs are called frogspawn and frogs lay them in water, in spring time.

Tadpoles

The eggs hatch and little tadpoles swim out. They have tails and live in water. **2**

Q. Where do tadpoles go to change into frogs?
A. A croak-room!

Super dad

Most frogs do not look after their babies. They lay eggs and swim away before they hatch.

Froglet

3 The tadpoles grow legs, and their tails shrink. They become froglets, and can leave the water.

This tree frog dad is carrying two baby tadpoles on his back.

LEARN A WORD:
metamorphosis
The change in body shape that happens during some animals' lives.

Puzzle time

Can you solve all the puzzles?

Tell us apart

There are three differences between Freddie and Frank – can you spot them?

Freddie

Frank

True or false?

1. A baby frog is called a tadpool.

2. Bullfrogs bellow when they are talking to their friends.

3. Frogs like living in wet places.

Rhyme time

Only four of these words rhyme with 'frog'. Can you find them?

dog fade fog four
pig pond log
mug clog splash

Count me in

Felix the frog usually eats ten spiders every day. One day Felix gives away half of his spiders to a hungry friend. How many spiders does Felix have left?

Who caught the fly?

Which of these frogs has caught a fly with her long, sticky tongue? Trace with your finger to find out.

Fiona

Felicity

Florence

Find the answers on page 2.

What noise do you make?

I make a very loud noise!

Frogs make lots of noises. We can croak, ribbit, sing, twitter, click and chirp.

Throat pouch is called a vocal sac

Q. What is a frog's favourite type of music?

A. Hip-hop!

Frog chorus

Male bullfrogs are large frogs with big vocal sacs. They make deep bellowing sounds to attract females.

I'm over here!

Male frogs make sounds to tell females where to find them. The sounds also tell other males to stay away.

Large ears detect sounds well

How do you stay safe?

I look scary!

My bright skin lets other animals know I am dangerous to eat. Birds, lizards and snakes eat frogs, but they stay away from me.

Poison dart frog

LEARN A WORD:
poisonous
Poisonous animals and plants are dangerous to eat or touch.

Don't eat me!

If a hungry animal
gets too close to
a fire-bellied toad
the toad will flash
its red belly, hoping
to scare it away.

Q. Why did the frog go to
hospital?

A. He needed a hop-eration!

Tree frog

Can you see me?

This frog is trying to
hide inside a flower. Do
you think the colour of
its skin helps it to
'disappear'?

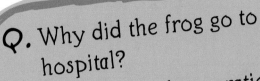

The frog prince

Use your stickers to illustrate the story.

Once upon a time, there was a rude and spoilt princess. One day she was playing with her ball in the garden. She threw it high in the air, and it landed with a splash in the well. The princess was cross. She kicked the side of the well and a large frog plopped out. Then the frog spoke – it croaked, "Why are you making so much noise?"

The princess ordered the frog to fetch her ball.

The frog leapt down the well and returned with the ball, but when the princess went to snatch it, the frog said, "Hasn't anyone taught you any manners? I have a request: I want to come and live in the palace, and eat off your plate, and sleep on your pillow, please."

The princess thought a promise to a frog wouldn't count, so she agreed. She took her ball and ran back to the palace. But her father the king said she must keep her word.

The princess sulked. She refused to eat her dinner with the frog sitting beside her. When bedtime came, she carried him to her room by one leg. She only let the frog sleep on the edge of her bed, while she did not sleep a wink all night.

On the second evening the princess ate

nothing again, and once more she did not sleep.

On the third night the princess was hungry, so she ate up all her dinner. At bedtime she was so tired that she fell deeply asleep.

The next morning the princess woke to find a handsome prince standing at the foot of her bed.

He told her that a fairy had turned him into a frog because he was spoilt. The spell could only be broken if someone just as rude was nice to him.

The princess learnt her lesson, and from that day forward she was much nicer. Before long, the princess and the prince were married and they lived happily ever after.

A retelling from the original story by the Brothers Grimm